Statistical Report of Crimes Against Volunteers 2012

Table of Contents

Contributors

Edward Hobson, *Associate Director for Safety and Security*

Daryl Sink, *Chief of Overseas Operations, Office of Safety and Security*

David Fleisig, *Lead Security Specialist, Office of Safety and Security*

Elizabeth Lowery, *Program Manager, Office of Safety and Security*

Jennifer Bingham, *Data Analyst, Office of Safety and Security*

Country Directors, Safety and Security Coordinators, Peace Corps Medical Officers, Peace Corps Safety and Security Officers, and Regional Security Advisors

Introduction

Purpose

The *Statistical Report of Crimes Against Volunteers 2012* provides summary statistics of reported crime incidents and Volunteer deaths for calendar year 2012. In addition, it also provides a global trend analysis of crime incidents over the last 10 years. The objective of this publication is to provide information regarding the number and types of crime incidents reported by Peace Corps Volunteers.

Measuring the Volunteer Population

The Volunteer population fluctuates throughout the year as new trainees arrive and seasoned Volunteers complete their service (normally 27 months). New Peace Corps posts are opening, while other posts may be suspending or closing operations. To more accurately compare crime data across posts, Volunteer/trainee years (VT years) are used in calculating crime incidence rates because this measurement provides a more accurate count of the actual length of time Volunteers are at risk of experiencing an incident (Appendix B). While there were 8,073 Volunteers and trainees serving as of September 30, 2012, there were only 8,046 VT years in calendar year 2012.

Overseas Post Changes

In calendar year 2012, Volunteers served in 70 Peace Corps posts in 76 countries. Programs that close or open within a calendar year only provide data for those months in which Volunteers actually served (see Appendix C).

Data Source

The data used to prepare this report was collected through the Crime Incident Reporting Form (CIRF) and the Consolidated Incident Reporting System (CIRS). The CIRS, an in-house developed application built using web services, was released in April 2008 and updated in August 2011.

Incident Classification

Crime incidents are ranked on a severity hierarchy ranging from Vandalism (least severe) to Death (most severe). Appendix A contains an overview of this hierarchy, including all definitions used to classify incidents. Information collected in the updated CIRS falls into one of eight categories, the first five of which are covered in this report:

- Sexual Assaults (rape/attempted rape, major sexual assault, and other sexual assault);

- Physical Assaults (kidnapping, aggravated assault, major physical assault, and other physical assault);

- Property Crimes (robbery, burglary, theft, and vandalism);

- Threats;

- Deaths (due to homicide, suicide, accident, natural cause, and indeterminate cause); and

- Other security incidents (including harassment and crimes in a Volunteer's community);

- Vehicular Accidents (including collisions, overturned vehicles, and pedestrians struck by vehicles);

- Crimes occurring to staff overseas.

The purposes of incident classification are to:

- Collect data that can inform applicants, invitees, Trainees and Volunteers on the types of incidents affecting Volunteers in each post; and

- Identify trends among reported incidents for the purposes of improving and directing Volunteer programs, training and support systems.

Regardless of how a crime is categorized, Volunteers have access to the same care and support services.

Peace Corps has recently adopted new classifications and definitions for several incident types including sexual assaults, physical assaults and property crimes, as well as creating a new incident type for stalking. These changes took effect on September 1, 2013.

An overview of the methodology utilized in preparing this report, as well as a discussion of incidence rates and data limitations, can be found in Appendix B.

Worldwide, Peace Corps Volunteers reported 1,582 crimes during 2012, or an overall incidence rate of 19.7 incidents per 100 VT years (Figure 1). Property crimes continue to be the most prevalent incidents reported (79.8 percent of all reported incidents), with thefts accounting for 49.2 percent of the overall total, burglaries 20.7 percent and robberies 9.8 percent. Of the more serious crimes reported, there were 15 aggravated assaults, 31 rapes/attempted rapes and 9 major sexual assaults.

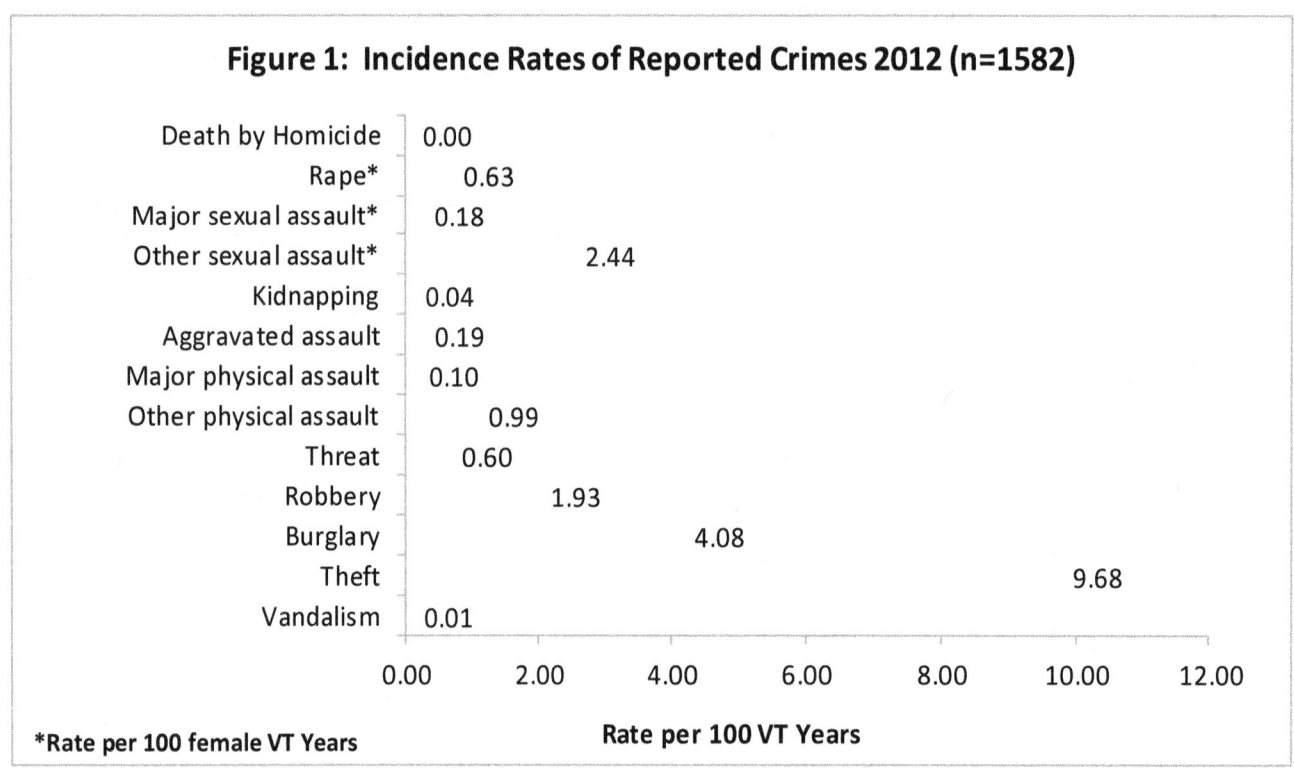

Figure 1: Incidence Rates of Reported Crimes 2012 (n=1582)

*Rate per 100 female VT Years

Definitions

Rape: Penetration of the vagina or anus with a penis, tongue, finger or object without the consent and/or against the will of the Volunteer. This includes when a victim is unable to consent because of ingestion of drugs and/or alcohol. Rape also includes forced oral sex, where:

1. the victim's mouth contacts the offender's genitals or anus, OR
2. the offender's mouth contacts the victim's genitals or anus, OR
3. the victim is forced to perform oral sex on another person.

Any unsuccessful attempts to penetrate the vagina or anus are also classified as rape.

Major sexual assault: Intentional or forced contact with the victim's breasts, genitals, mouth, buttocks, or anus OR disrobing of the Volunteer or offender without contact of the Volunteer's aforementioned body parts, for sexual gratification AND any of the following:

1. the use of a weapon by the offender, OR
2. physical injury to the victim, OR
3. when the victim has to use *substantial* force to disengage the offender.

Other sexual assault: Unwanted or forced kissing, fondling, and/or groping of the breasts, genitals, mouth, buttocks, or anus for sexual gratification.

Sexual Assaults

The following section provides a global analysis of sexual assault incidents. Incidence of sexual assault is expressed as incidents reported by females per 100 female VT years because women are at a much greater risk for sexual assaults than men. In 2012, 97.6 percent of the sexual assaults reported worldwide were against female Volunteers. Use of female-specific incidence rates better characterizes the risk of sexual assault. In comparing year-to-year data for rapes/attempted rapes and major sexual assaults, incidence rates should be interpreted with caution due to the relatively small number of reported incidents perpetrated annually against Peace Corps Volunteers.

Arrest and prosecutorial outcomes for reported sexual assaults are also detailed below. An important note about outcome data: in the year 2012, the Consolidated Incident Reporting System functioned as a point-in-time record. Not all incidents are updated as the case progresses.

I. Rape/Attempted Rape

Global Analysis

Table 1 provides the number and rates of rapes/attempted rapes reported by female Volunteers. As noted above, only sexual assaults reported by female Volunteers are included in the table and graph; however, incidents occurring to male Volunteers are noted in the text for each incident type.

Table 1: Summary—Rape/ Attempted Rape	
Incidents reported by female Volunteers only	
2012 Number of Incidents	31
2012 Incidence Rate (per 100 Female VT years)	0.63
2011 Number of Incidents	38
2011 Incidence Rate (per 100 Female VT years)	0.72
Yearly Rate Comparison (2011 to 2012)	-13%
10-Year Rate Comparison (2003 to 2012)	-5%

There were 31 rapes/attempted rapes reported by female Peace Corps Volunteers worldwide during 2012, resulting in an incidence rate of 0.63 incidents per 100 female VT years. The incidence rate for rapes/attempted rapes remained relatively unchanged from 2003 to 2008. In 2009, a substantially lower number was reported,

though in 2010 this number returned to the level previously seen. In 2011, the number and rate climbed to the highest level seen since 2003, potentially as a result of increased media coverage and/or new reporting and response procedures and additional training instituted throughout the year (Figure 2). In 2012, the number and rate declined, though the rate is still higher than the 10-year average of 0.55 incidents per 100 female VT years. Male Peace Corps Volunteers did not report any rapes/attempted rapes during 2012.

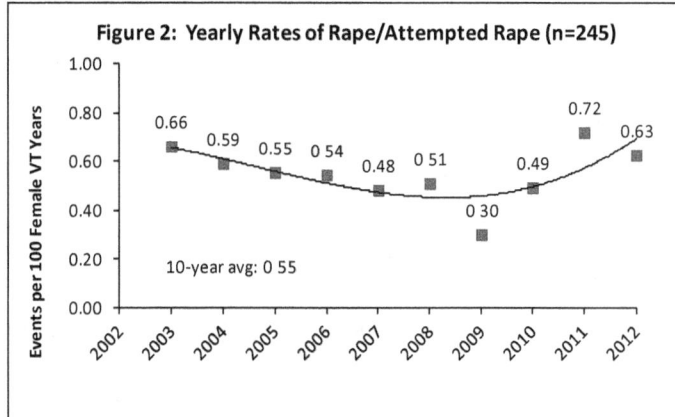

Figure 2: Yearly Rates of Rape/Attempted Rape (n=245)

Outcomes

Volunteers in 7 of the 31 reported rape/attempted rape incidents chose to report to local authorities. Of those, 2 Volunteers later chose not to pursue the case and 5 are still under investigation or in the judicial process. Offenders have been apprehended in 3 of the incidents. As of the date of this report, no verdicts have been rendered.

II. Major Sexual Assault

Global Analysis

Table 2 provides the number and rates of major sexual assaults reported by female Volunteers.

Table 2: Summary—Major Sexual Assault	
Incidents reported by female Volunteers only	
2012 Number of Incidents	9
2012 Incidence Rate (per 100 Female VT years)	0.18
2011 Number of Incidents	14
2011 Incidence Rate (per 100 Female VT years)	0.27
Yearly Rate Comparison (2011 to 2012)	-31%
10-Year Rate Comparison (2003 to 2012)	-33%

There were 9 major sexual assaults reported by female Peace Corps Volunteers worldwide during 2012, resulting in an incidence rate of 0.18 incidents per 100 female VT years. Over the last 10-year period, the rate of major sexual assaults has varied, with 2012 representing the lowest rate of reported incidents in the 10-year period(Figure 3). Male Peace Corps Volunteers did not report any major sexual assaults during 2012.

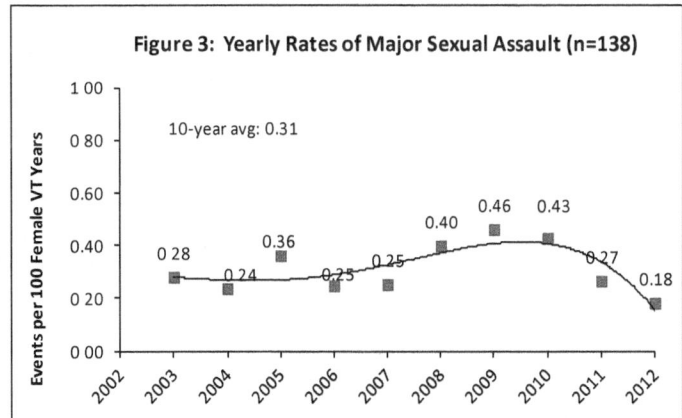

Figure 3: Yearly Rates of Major Sexual Assault (n=138)

Outcomes

Volunteers in 6 of the 9 reported major sexual assault incidents chose to report to local authorities. Of those, 5 are still under investigation or in the judicial process. Offenders have been apprehended in 3 of the incidents. As of the date of this report, 1 guilty verdict has been rendered.

III. Other Sexual Assault

Global Analysis

Table 3 provides the number and rates for other sexual assaults reported by female Volunteers.

Table 3: Summary—Other Sexual Assault	
Incidents reported by female Volunteers only	
2012 Number of Incidents	121
2012 Incidence Rate (per 100 Female VT years)	2.44
2011 Number of Incidents	94
2011 Incidence Rate (per 100 Female VT years)	1.78
Yearly Rate Comparison (2011 to 2012)	37%
10-Year Rate Comparison (2003 to 2012)	78%

There were 121 other sexual assaults reported by Peace Corps Volunteers worldwide during 2012, resulting in an incidence rate of 2.44 incidents per 100 female VT years. This number and rate are the highest reported in the 10-year period. Until 2012, the rate routinely fluctuated around an average of 1.70 incidents per 100 female VT years (Figure 4). Male Peace Corps Volunteers reported 4 other sexual assaults worldwide in 2012, resulting in an incidence rate of 0.13 incidents per 100 male VT years.

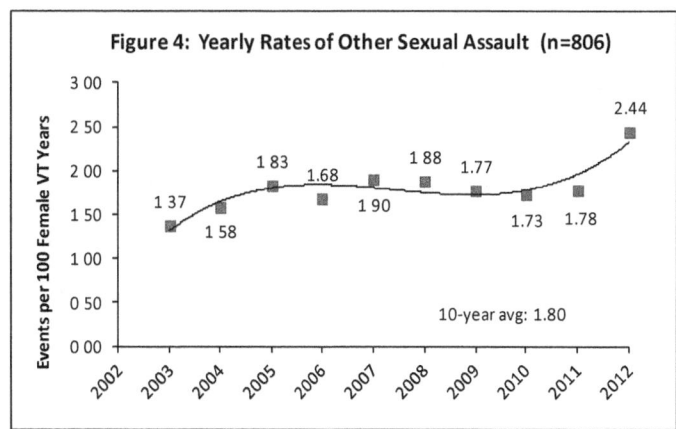

Figure 4: Yearly Rates of Other Sexual Assault (n=806)

Outcomes

Volunteers in 19 of the 125 reported other sexual assault incidents chose to report to local authorities. Of those, 7 Volunteers later chose not to pursue the case and 10 are still under investigation or in the judicial process. Offenders have been apprehended in 7 of the incidents. As of the date of this report, 2 guilty verdicts have been rendered.

Definitions

Kidnapping: The unlawful seizure, transportation, and/or detention of a victim against her/his will for ransom or reward. This category includes hostage-taking.

Aggravated assault: Attack or threat of attack with a weapon in a manner capable of inflicting severe bodily injury or death. Attack without a weapon or object when severe bodily injury results. Severe bodily injury includes broken bones, lost teeth, internal injuries, severe laceration, loss of consciousness, or any injury requiring two or more days of hospitalization. Attempted murder should be reported as aggravated assault.

Major physical assault: Aggressive contact that requires the Volunteer to use substantial force to disengage the offender OR that results in major bodily injury, including any of the following: injury requiring less than two days of hospitalization; or diagnostic X-rays to rule out broken bones (and no fracture is found); or surgical intervention (including stitches).

Other physical assault: Aggressive contact that does not require the Volunteer to use substantial force to disengage the offender and results in no injury or only minor injury. Minor injury does not require hospitalization, X-ray or surgical intervention (including stitches).

The following section provides a global analysis of all physical assault incidents. Incidence of physical assaults is expressed per 100 VT years.

Physical assault definitions have undergone several changes in the past few years which make long-term trend monitoring difficult. Prior to 2006, robbery was defined as an incident devoid of violence or threat of violence in which property or cash is taken directly from a Volunteer. If the robbery was accompanied by an attack, the robbery would have been reported as a physical assault. Some incidents that would have been classified as aggravated assaults, major physical assaults, or other physical assaults prior to 2006 are now classified as robberies, leading to a general decline in the physical assault rates and an increase in robbery rates since 2006.

The next change involved only physical assaults. Incidents involving any type of weapon use or threat are classified as aggravated assaults prior to 2009, including children throwing small rocks or threats made with plastic bottles. Since that time, assaults involving weapons are classified on the basis of the potential of the weapon to cause severe bodily injury or death (aggravated assaults), major bodily injury (major physical assault), or no injury to minor injury (other physical assault).

Arrest and prosecutorial outcomes for reported physical assaults are also detailed below. An important note about outcome data: in the year 2012, the Consolidated Incident Reporting System functioned as a point-in-time record. Not all incidents are updated as the case progresses.

I. Kidnapping

Global Analysis

Kidnapping was added to the list of reportable incidents in 2006, but there were no kidnapping incidents reported in 2006 or 2007. Two incidents were reported in each of 2008 and 2009; however, in 2010 and 2011 the number reported returned to zero. In 2012, three incidents were reported as kidnappings for an incidence rate of 0.03 incidents per 100 VT years. Due to these low numbers, no table or chart is shown for kidnapping incidents.

Two of the reported incidents involved Volunteers using transportation. In both cases, a Volunteer entered a ve-

hicle with a final destination in mind. The driver began to make advances and refused to stop the car or let the Volunteer leave when asked. In both cases, the Volunteer was taken to her originally requested destination, though both trips took longer than is considered normal.

In the final reported kidnapping, a former girlfriend of a Volunteer invited him to her home and locked him in a room in order to convince him to stay with her. The Volunteer was only allowed to leave after more than an hour had passed.

Outcomes

Volunteers in 1 of the 3 reported kidnapping incidents chose to report to local authorities. This case is still under investigation.

II. Aggravated Assault

Global Analysis

Table 4 provides the number and rates of aggravated assaults.

Table 4: Summary—Aggravated Assault	
2012 Number of Incidents	15
2012 Incidence Rate (per 100 VT years)	0.19
2011 Number of Incidents	17
2011 Incidence Rate (per 100 VT years)	0.20
Yearly Rate Comparison (2011 to 2012)	-5%
7-Year Rate Comparison (2006 to 2012)	-64%

There were 15 aggravated assaults reported by Peace Corps Volunteers worldwide during 2012, resulting in an incidence rate of 0.19 incidents per 100 VT years. The aggravated assault number and rate have declined in the last 10 years, though the rate has been relatively stable during any period in which the definition remains consistent.

The overall decline in aggravated assaults since 2003 likely reflects the two changes made to the definition in the past 10 years. Aggravated assault rates have remained relatively unchanged since 2009, the year of the second definition change (Figure 5).

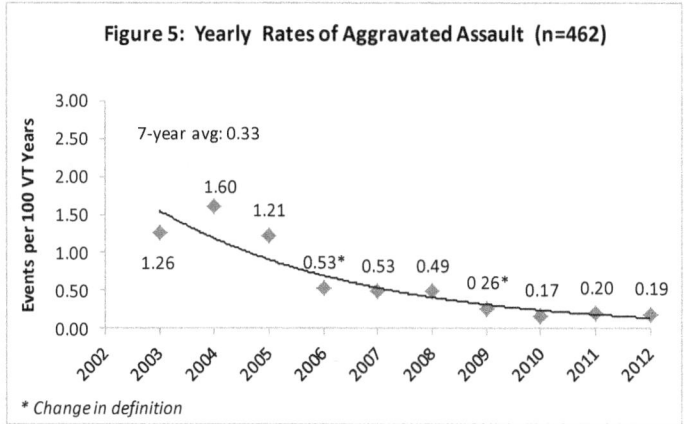

Figure 5: Yearly Rates of Aggravated Assault (n=462)

7-year avg: 0.33

1.26 1.60 1.21 0.53* 0.53 0.49 0 26* 0.17 0.20 0.19

Change in definition

Outcomes

Volunteers in 9 of the 15 reported aggravated assault incidents chose to report to local authorities. Of those, 3 Volunteers later chose not to pursue the case and 5 are still under investigation or in the judicial process. Offenders have been apprehended in 1 incident. As of the date of this report, 1 guilty verdict has been rendered.

III. Major Physical Assault

Global Analysis

Table 5 provides the number and rates of major physical assaults.

Table 5: Summary—Major Physical Assault	
2012 Number of Incidents	8
2012 Incidence Rate (per 100 VT years)	0.10
2011 Number of Incidents	6
2011 Incidence Rate (per 100 VT years)	0.07
Yearly Rate Comparison (2011 to 2012)	44%
7-Year Rate Comparison (2006 to 2012)	-23%

There were 8 major physical assaults reported by Peace Corps Volunteers worldwide during 2012, resulting in an incidence rate of 0.10 incidents per 100 VT years.

The decline in major physical assaults from 2005 to 2006 reflects the definition change. Between 2006 and 2009, the rate for major physical assaults showed no clear di-

rectional trend, followed by a decrease in 2011 and 2012, likely as a result of the second change in definition (Figure 6).

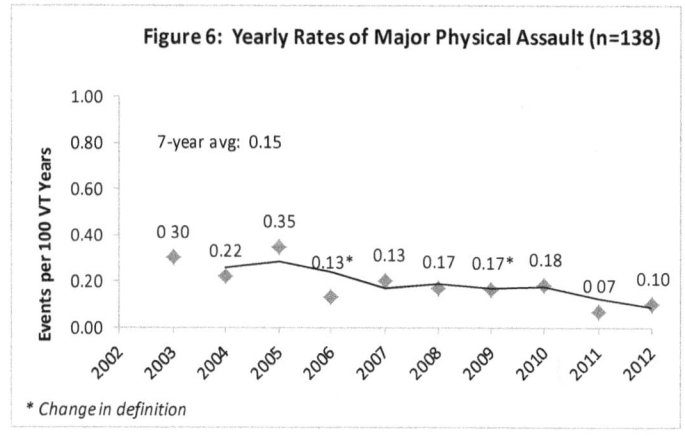

Figure 6: Yearly Rates of Major Physical Assault (n=138)

7-year avg: 0.15

0 30 0.22 0.35 0.13* 0.13 0.17 0.17* 0.18 0 07 0.10

Change in definition

Outcomes

Volunteers in 6 of the 8 reported major physical assault incidents chose to report to local authorities. Of those, 1 Volunteer later chose not to pursue the case and 5 are still under investigation or in the judicial process. Offenders have been apprehended in 3 of the incidents. As of the date of this report, no verdicts have been rendered.

IV. Other Physical Assault

Global Analysis

Table 6 provides the number and rates of other physical assaults.

Table 6: Summary—Other Physical Assault	
2012 Number of Incidents	80
2012 Incidence Rate (per 100 VT years)	0.99
2011 Number of Incidents	79
2011 Incidence Rate (per 100 VT years)	0.91
Yearly Rate Comparison (2011 to 2012)	9%
7-Year Rate Comparison (2006 to 2012)	71%

There were 80 other physical assault incidents reported

by Peace Corps Volunteers worldwide during 2012, resulting in a rate of 0.99 incidents per 100 VT years.

The decline in other physical assaults in 2006 reflects the definition change. Since 2006, the incidence rate for other physical assaults shows an upward trend. This trend continued in 2012, likely as a result of the second definition change, which classified previous aggravated assaults as other physical assaults when the likelihood of severe bodily injury from use of a weapon is low (Figure 7).

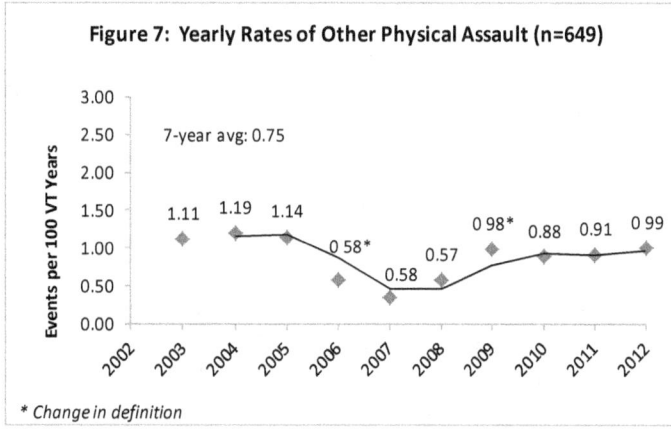

Figure 7: Yearly Rates of Other Physical Assault (n=649)

7-year avg: 0.75

Change in definition

Outcomes

Volunteers in 38 of the 80 reported other physical assault incidents chose to report to local authorities. Of those, 10 Volunteers later chose not to pursue the case and 27 are still under investigation or in the judicial process. Offenders have been apprehended in 16 of the incidents. As of the date of this report, no verdicts have been rendered.

Threats

Definitions

Threat: A threat is made without physical contact or injury to the Volunteer. Threat occurs when the Volunteer is placed in reasonable fear of bodily harm through the use of threatening words and/or other conduct. This offense includes stalking and may be determined by the perception of the Volunteer.

The following section provides a global analysis of all threat incidents. Incidence of threats is expressed per 100 VT years.

Arrest and prosecutorial outcomes for reported threats are detailed below. An important note about outcome data: in the year 2012, the Consolidated Incident Reporting System functioned as a point-in-time record. Not all incidents are updated as the case progresses.

I. Threat

Global Analysis

Table 7 provides the number and rates of threats.

Table 7: Summary—Threat	
2012 Number of Incidents	48
2012 Incidence Rate (per 100 VT years)	0.60
2011 Number of Incidents	52
2011 Incidence Rate (per 100 VT years)	0.60
Yearly Rate Comparison (2011 to 2012)	-1%
7-Year Rate Comparison (2006 to 2012)	-29%

There were 48 threat incidents reported by Peace Corps Volunteers worldwide during 2012, resulting in a rate of 0.60 incidents per 100 VT years.

It is important to note that prior to 2006, only death threats were a reportable category. Beginning in 2006, a new class of threats known as "intimidation" were added as a reportable category, resulting in a substantial increase in numbers. Due to this change in reporting practice, the trend graph shows only the 7-year period covered in this report. The incidence rate for threats has been highly variable, reaching its peak in 2008, followed by its lowest point in 2011 and 2012 (Figure 8).

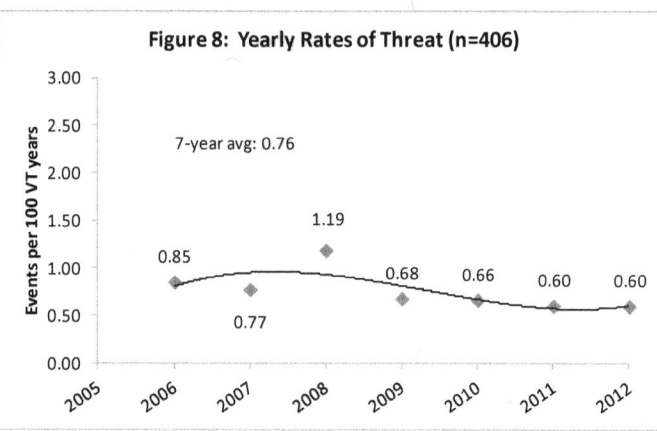

Figure 8: Yearly Rates of Threat (n=406)

Outcomes

Volunteers in 22 of the 48 reported threat incidents chose to report to local authorities. Of those, 8 Volunteers later chose not to pursue the case and 12 are under investigation or in the judicial process. Offenders have been apprehended in 5 of the incidents. As of the date of this report, 1 guilty verdict and 1 not guilty verdict have been rendered.

Property Crimes

Definitions

Robbery: The taking or attempting to take anything of value under confrontational circumstances from the control, custody or care of the Volunteer by force or threat of force or violence and/or by putting the victim in fear of immediate harm. Also includes when a robber displays/uses a weapon or transports the Volunteer to obtain his/her money or possessions.

Burglary with Assault: Unlawful or forcible entry of a Volunteer's residence accompanied by an Other Sexual Assault or Other Physical Assault. Also includes illegal entry of a hotel room accompanied by an Other Sexual Assault or Other Physical Assault.

Burglary—No Assault: Unlawful or forcible entry of a Volunteer's residence. This incident type usually, but not always, involves theft. As long as the person entering has no legal right to be present in the residence, a burglary has occurred. Also includes illegal entry of a hotel room.

Theft: The taking away of or attempt to take away property or cash without involving force or illegal entry. Includes pickpocketing, stolen purses, and thefts from a residence that do not involve an illegal entry.

Vandalism: Mischievous or malicious defacement, destruction, or damage of property.

Property Crimes

The following section provides a global analysis of all property crime incidents. Incidence of property crimes is expressed per 100 VT years.

Arrest and prosecutorial outcomes for reported property crimes are detailed below. An important note about outcome data: in the year 2012, the Consolidated Incident Reporting System functioned as a point-in-time record. Not all incidents are updated as the case progresses. Due to the small number of reported incidents, outcomes for vandalism are not analyzed.

I. Robbery

Global Analysis

Table 8 provides the number and rates of robberies.

Table 8: Summary—Robbery	
2012 Number of Incidents	155
2012 Incidence Rate (per 100 VT years)	1.93
2011 Number of Incidents	188
2011 Incidence Rate (per 100 VT years)	2.17
Yearly Rate Comparison (2011 to 2012)	-11%
7-Year Rate Comparison (2006 to 2012)	-18%

There were 155 robberies reported by Peace Corps Volunteers worldwide during 2012, resulting in a rate of 1.93 incidents per 100 VT years.

As noted in the physical assaults section, prior to 2006, incidents that would have been categorized as physical assaults in previous years are now classified as robberies, resulting in an increase in the incidence rate from 2005 to 2006 (Figure 9). Since 2006, the incidence rate for robberies has declined, with a peak in 2010.

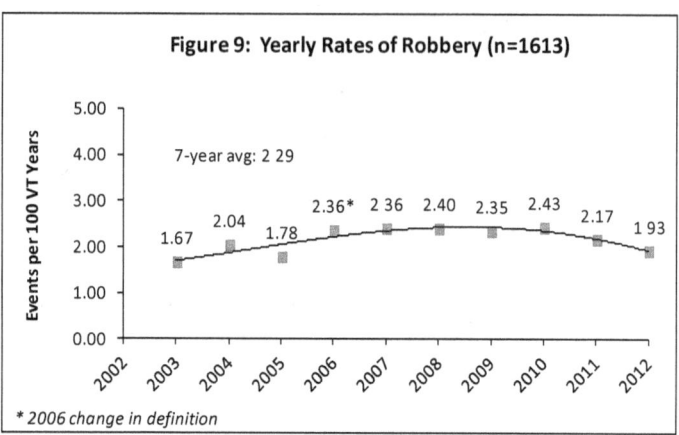

Figure 9: Yearly Rates of Robbery (n=1613)

7-year avg: 2 29

1.67, 2.04, 1.78, 2.36*, 2 36, 2.40, 2.35, 2.43, 2.17, 1 93

* 2006 change in definition

Outcomes

Volunteers in 99 of the 155 reported robbery incidents chose to report to local authorities. Of those, 15 Volunteers later chose not to pursue the case and 82 are still under investigation or have entered the judicial process. In 1 incident, the state declined to investigate. Offenders have been apprehended in 10 of the incidents. As of the date of this report, no verdicts have been rendered.

II. Burglary

Global Analysis

Table 9 provides the number and rates of burglaries.

Table 9: Summary—Burglary	
2012 Number of Incidents	328
2012 Incidence Rate (per 100 VT years)	4.08
2011 Number of Incidents	345
2011 Incidence Rate (per 100 VT years)	3.98
Yearly Rate Comparison (2011 to 2012)	2%
10-Year Rate Comparison (2003 to 2012)	55%

There were 328 burglaries reported by Peace Corps Volunteers worldwide during 2012, resulting in a rate of 4.08 incidents per 100 VT years. Beginning in 2009, burglaries were categorized as either "with assault" or "no assault." Only 6 burglaries were reported as burglary with assault in 2012, for an incidence rate of 0.07 incidents per 100 VT years. The total burglary rate for 2012 was a slight increase over 2011. The incidence rate for burglaries appears to have peaked in 2009, at 4.72 incidents per 100 VT years, and has displayed a downward trend in the years since (Figure 10).

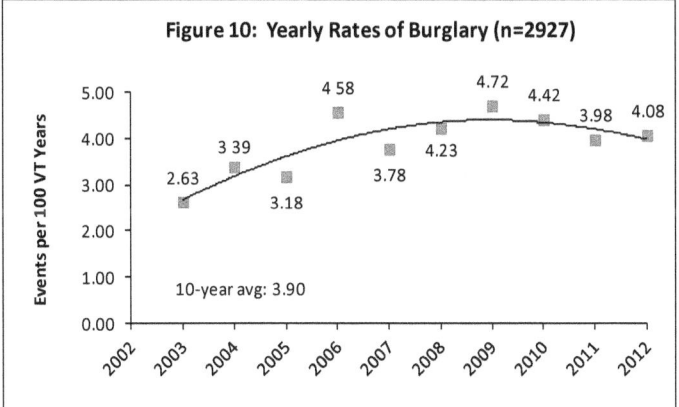

Figure 10: Yearly Rates of Burglary (n=2927)

10-year avg: 3.90

Outcomes

Volunteers in 221 of the 328 reported burglary incidents chose to report to local authorities. Of those, 25 Volunteers later chose not to pursue the case and 192 are still under investigation or have entered the judicial process. Offenders have been apprehended in 28 of the incidents. As of the date of this report, 3 guilty verdict and 1 not guilty verdict have been rendered.

III. Theft

Global Analysis

Table 10 provides the number and rates of thefts.

Table 10: Summary—Theft	
2012 Number of Incidents	779
2012 Incidence Rate (per 100 VT years)	9.68
2011 Number of Incidents	859
2011 Incidence Rate (per 100 VT years)	9.92
Yearly Rate Comparison (2011 to 2012)	-2%
10-Year Rate Comparison (2003 to 2012)	31%

There were 779 thefts reported by Peace Corps Volunteers worldwide during 2012, resulting in a rate of 9.68

incidents per 100 VT years. Reported thefts have increased overall in the 10-year period.

Reported thefts have generally increased over the past 10 years, and between 2003 and 2012, the rate of thefts increased by 31 percent. (Figure 11). Although it is difficult to say with certainty, the theft incidence rate appears to be stabilizing following many years of steady increase. While the causes for this are not yet known, possible reasons include: among Volunteers, there may be increased knowledge regarding the reporting process, as well as growing confidence and trust in staff, particularly safety and security staff, at post.

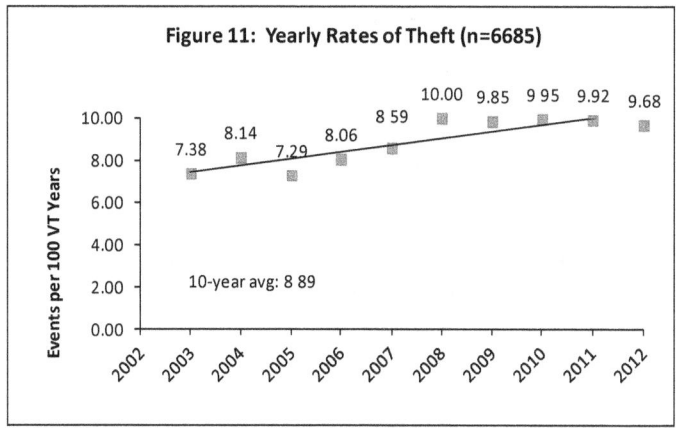

Figure 11: Yearly Rates of Theft (n=6685)

10-year avg: 8 89

Outcomes

Volunteers in 424 of the 779 reported theft incidents chose to report to local authorities. Of those, 93 Volunteers later chose not to pursue the case and 324 are still under investigation or have entered the judicial process. In 7 incidents, the state declined to investigate Offenders have been apprehended in 15 of the incidents. As of the date of this report, no verdicts have been rendered.

IV. Vandalism

Global Analysis

Table 11 provides the number and rates of vandalism.

Table 11: Summary—Vandalism	
2012 Number of Incidents	1
2012 Incidence Rate (per 100 VT years)	0.01
2011 Number of Incidents	7
2011 Incidence Rate (per 100 VT years)	0.08
Yearly Rate Comparison (2011 to 2012)	-85%
10-Year Rate Comparison (2003 to 2012)	-97%

There was 1 vandalism incident reported by Peace Corps Volunteers worldwide during 2012, resulting in a rate of 0.01 incidents per 100 VT years. The rate of vandalism has fluctuated since 2002, though reports of this crime are steadily decreasing (Figure 12).

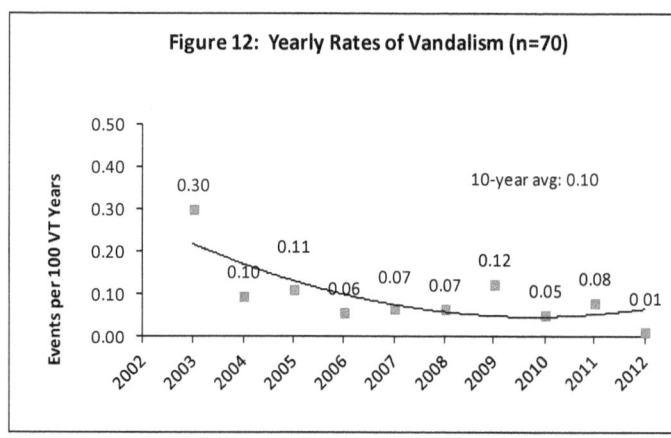

Figure 12: Yearly Rates of Vandalism (n=70)

Definitions

Volunteer Deaths by:

Homicide: The willful (non-negligent) killing of a Volunteer by another person. Deaths caused by negligence, suicides and accidental deaths are excluded.

Suicide: The act of a Volunteer killing him/herself intentionally.

Accident: Death of a Volunteer due to unintentional injury.

Natural cause: Death of a Volunteer due to illness or natural causes.

Indeterminate cause: Death of a Volunteer pending further investigation to establish cause of death. Deaths categorized as this type will be updated after 6 months and re-categorized as death due to homicide, suicide, accident or natural cause.

Volunteer death encompasses the categories of: homicide, suicide, accidental death, death due to natural causes, and/or death due to indeterminate causes.

From 1961 through the end of 2012, there have been 23 homicides in the Peace Corps. In 2012, there was 1 in-service death due to natural causes. In the five-year period from 2008 to 2012, there were 13 Volunteer deaths: 6 accidental deaths, 2 homicides, and 5 deaths due to natural causes. A summary table and figures for in-service deaths are not provided because the small number of deaths does not allow for meaningful analysis.

Appendices

Death by Homicide > Kidnapping > Rape > Major Sexual Assault > Robbery > Aggravated Assault > Major Physical Assault > Burglary with Assault > Other Sexual Assault > Other Physical Assault > Burglary – No Assault> Threat > Theft > Vandalism

Death by Homicide	• The willful (non-negligent) killing of one human being by another • Deaths caused by negligence, suicides, and accidental deaths are excluded
Kidnapping	• Unlawful seizure and/or detention of a Volunteer against his/her will for ransom or reward • Includes hostage-taking
Rape	• Penetration of the vagina or anus with a penis, tongue, finger or object without the consent and/or against the will of the victim • Includes when a victim is unable to consent because of ingestion of drugs and/or alcohol • Includes forced oral sex and any unsuccessful attempts to penetrate the vagina or anus

Major Sexual Assault	• Intentional or forced contact with the breasts, genitals, mouth, buttocks, or anus <u>OR</u> disrobing of the Volunteer or offender without bodily contact
	
	• <u>AND</u> any of the following:
	
	    1. the use of a weapon by the assailant, OR
	
	    2. physical injury to the victim OR
	
	    3. when the victim has to use substantial force to disengage the assailant

Robbery	• The taking or attempting to take anything of value under confrontational circumstances from the control, custody or care of another person by force, threat of force, violence, and/or by putting the victim in fear of immediate harm • Also includes when a robber displays/uses a weapon or transports the Volunteer to obtain his/her money or possessions
Aggravated Assault	• Attack or threat of attack with a weapon in a manner capable of causing severe bodily injury or death • Attack without a weapon when severe bodily injury results. • Severe bodily injury includes: broken bones, lost teeth, internal injuries, severe laceration, loss of consciousness, or any injury requiring two or more days of hospitalization
Major Physical Assault	• Aggressive contact that requires the Volunteer to use substantial force to disengage the offender or that results in major bodily injury • Major bodily injury includes: injury requiring less than two days of hospitalization, OR diagnostic X-rays to rule out broken bones (and no fracture is found), OR surgical intervention (including suturing)

Appendix A: Severity Hierarchy and Incident Definitions

Burglary with Assault	• Unlawful or forcible entry of a Volunteer's residence accompanied by an other sexual assault or other physical assault • The illegal entry may be forcible, such as breaking a window or slashing a screen, or may be without force by entering through an unlocked door or an open window • Also includes illegal entry of a hotel room
Other Sexual Assault	• Unwanted or forced kissing, fondling, and/or groping of the breasts, genitals, mouth, buttocks, or anus for sexual gratification
Other Physical Assault	• Aggressive contact that does not require the Volunteer to use substantial force to disengage the offender and results in no injury or only minor injury • Minor injury does not require hospitalization, X-ray or surgical intervention (including stitches)
Burglary—No Assault	• Unlawful or forcible entry of a Volunteer's residence • This crime usually, but not always, involves theft • The illegal entry may be forcible, such as breaking a window or slashing a screen, or may be without force by entering through an unlocked door or an open window • Also includes illegal entry of a hotel room
Threat	• When the Volunteer is placed in reasonable fear of bodily harm through the use of threatening words and/or other conduct • This offense includes stalking and may be determined by the perception of the Volunteer
Theft	• The taking away of or attempt to take away property or cash without involving force or illegal entry • There is no known direct contact with the victim • Includes pick-pocketing, stolen purses, and thefts from a residence that do not involve an illegal entry
Vandalism	• Mischievous or malicious defacement, destruction, or damage of property
Other Security Incident	• Any situation that directly impacts the security of a Volunteer but that does not meet any of the definitions of a crime

The Peace Corps uses a hierarchy rule in classifying incidents, similar to that used by the Federal Bureau of Investigation in its Uniform Crime Reporting system. When a single offense is committed, the incident is classified according to the details of that offense. However, in multiple-offense situations, the hierarchy rule requires that the reporter locate the classification that is highest on the severity hierarchy and report the entire incident using that classification, rather than multiple, less-severe classifications. This does not affect the charges that an offender may incur according to local law.

Appendix B: Methodology

Data Analysis

The Crime Statistics and Analysis Unit within the Office of Safety and Security conducts a multi-step quality-assurance process to mitigate errors inherent to the data collection process (i.e., respondent errors, non-response errors, misclassifications, etc.). Each report received at headquarters is reviewed for: 1) appropriate crime classification; and 2) discrepancies between the summary and the closed-ended questions (i.e., questions with multiple choice responses). Data are reviewed daily for misclassification, inconsistencies, errors or missing data and are sent back to the submitter for correction or clarification.

The *Statistical Report of Crimes Against Volunteers 2012* displays data from five categories of reported incidents occurring to Volunteers: sexual assaults, physical assaults, threats, property crimes, and Volunteer deaths. Incidence rates and global trend analyses are provided in each of the four largest categories. This report includes three periods of data collection and analysis: the 2012 calendar year, the 7-year period from 2006-2012, and the 10-year period from 2003-2012. Analyzing multiple time periods provides a better understanding of areas of fluctuation and long-standing crime trends. Data for this report are current as of March 14, 2013. Longitudinal data are represented in scatter plots that provide crime incidence rates for each year. Within each scatter plot, a trend line approximates the best-fit line through the data points.

Incidence Rates

$$\text{Incidence Rate} = (\text{Number of reported incidents}/\text{VT Years}) \times 100$$

Incidence rates are more accurate indicators of reported crimes for comparative purposes than the raw number of incidents, or the crime volume. By reporting incidence rates (i.e., the number of incidents as a function of the number of Volunteers serving in a given post over time), more meaningful comparisons can be made across Peace Corps posts or regions that have differing numbers of Volunteers. For example, 25 reported incidents of aggravated assault affect a higher percentage of Volunteers at a post with 100 Volunteers than a post with 200 Volunteers.

Furthermore, incidence rates are calculated using VT years, which are more accurate than using the number of Volunteers in the denominator. The VT year calculation considers the length of time Volunteers were at risk; or, the length of time served by Volunteers. A VT year encompasses the amount of time a Volunteer/trainee served during a given year between the start of domestic training ("staging") through the end of service. For example, if a Volunteer leaves after six months, he or she is only at risk during that six-month period, and only half (0.5) of a VT year is contributed to the incidence rate denominator. If a Volunteer stays the full year, one full (1.0) VT year is contributed. Unless otherwise noted in the report, incidence rates are reported as incidents per 100 Volunteer/trainee (VT) years.

Data Limitations

There are three limitations to interpreting the data in this report that the reader should bear in mind.

The first limitation relates to the selective reporting of security incidents by Volunteers. In reviewing the frequency of incidents, the reader should keep in mind that these are the numbers for *reported* incidents. Victimization and Volunteer survey findings consistently show that underreporting of crimes does occur. Related to the self-reported nature of the incident reporting process is the potential for misclassification of incidents. Incidents are classified solely on the information provided by the Volunteer, which could lead to inaccurate classification if a Volunteer does not provide all necessary and relevant information. The incident definitions are included in Appendix A.

The second limitation is more of a cautionary note and relates to comparing incidence rates across Peace Corps posts.

Appendix B: Methodology

While the use of incidence rates does allow for comparisons across posts, caution should be used when comparing crime rates for posts with limited VT years, such as Honduras (19 VT years), because they appear dramatically higher when compared to rates for posts with greater VT years, such as Zambia (283 VT years), even when the number of incidents is small. To illustrate, an increase from one theft to two thefts at a post with 25 VT years results in the theft incidence rate increasing from 4.0 to 8.0 incidents per 100 VT years. Whereas, with a large post with 175 VT years, the theft incidence rate would increase from 0.6 to 1.1 per 100 VT years. In 2012, there were 12 posts (17 percent) with fewer than 50 VT years. In addition, rates based on a small number of incidents (fewer than 30), such as aggravated assault, should be interpreted with caution as they may not be an accurate indicator of risk. Appendix E provides the number of reported incidents and the number of VT years contributed by each post in 2012.

A third limitation involves the analysis of the data by the Volunteer's post of service. The vast majority of incidents occur in the Volunteer's post of service. However, incidents against Volunteers do happen outside their post of service; for example, when a Volunteer is vacationing in another country. The percentage of incidents occurring outside the Volunteer's post of service is typically 3 percent or less (Appendix F).

Appendix C: Peace Corps Posts and Regions (2012)

Africa	Europe, Mediterranean and Asia	Inter-America and the Pacific
Benin	Albania	Belize
Botswana	Armenia	Colombia
Burkina Faso	Azerbaijan	Costa Rica
Cameroon	Bulgaria	Dominican Republic
Cape Verde***	Cambodia	Eastern Caribbean
Ethiopia	China	Ecuador
Ghana	Georgia	El Salvador
Guinea	Indonesia	Fiji
Kenya	Jordan	Guatemala
Lesotho	Kyrgyz Republic	Guyana
Liberia	Macedonia	Honduras*
Madagascar	Moldova	Jamaica
Malawi	Mongolia	Mexico
Mali*	Morocco	Micronesia
Mozambique	Nepal**	Nicaragua
Namibia	Philippines	Panama
Niger*	Romania	Paraguay
Rwanda	Thailand	Peru
Senegal	Turkmenistan***	Samoa
Sierra Leone	Ukraine	Suriname
South Africa		Tonga
Swaziland		Vanuatu
Tanzania		
The Gambia		
Togo		
Uganda		
Zambia		

*	Peace Corps posts suspended:	Honduras, Mali, Niger
**	Peace Corps posts opened or reopened:	Nepal
***	Peace Corps posts closed:	Cape Verde, Turkmenistan

Note: Programs noted above do not provide data for a full calendar year, so incidence of security events for this post should be interpreted cautiously.

Demographic Characteristic	N	%
Men	3,084	38
Women	4,989	62
Racial Minority Volunteers/Trainees	1,618	22
Seniors (50+)	586	7
Oldest Volunteer	82	
Age: Average/Median/Most Common	27.5/24/22	
Age:		
<20	2	<1
20-29	6,796	84
30-39	547	7
40-49	142	2
50-59	217	3
60-69	332	4
70-79	35	<1
80-89	2	<1
Ethnicity:		
Caucasian	5,854	78
Hispanic	617	8
Asian American	378	5
African American	362	5
Mixed Ethnicity	252	3
Native American	9	<1
Not Specified	601	N/A

Demographic Characteristic	N	%
Marital status:		
Single	6,928	86
Married	564	7
Divorced	365	5
Engaged	74	<1
Married/serving alone	79	<1
Widowed	62	<1
Married/while serving	1	<1
Educational level:		
No High School Diploma/Other	2	<1
High School Diploma	12	<1
1-2 years college	18	<1
Technical School Graduate	10	<1
AA Degree	38	<1
3 years college	309	5
Bachelor's Degree	5,225	80
Graduate Study	76	1
Graduate Degree	856	13
Not Specified	1,527	

Notes:

1. As reported on September 30, 2012.
2. N = Volunteers in the field. Reported by the Peace Corps' Office of Strategic Information, Research, and Planning.
3. Some percentages do not add to 100 due to rounding.

Appendix E: Global, Regional, and Post Crime Numbers and Rates (2012)

Sexual Assault Events and Incidence Rates (2012)

Global

All Posts	Female VT Years	Rape		Major Sexual Assault		Other Sexual Assault		All Sexual Assault	
		Events	Rate	Events	Rate	Events	Rate	Events	Rate
	4954	31	0.63	9	0.18	125	2.52	165	3.33

Africa Region

Posts	Female VT Years	Rape		Major Sexual Assault		Other Sexual Assault		All Sexual Assault	
		Events	Rate	Events	Rate	Events	Rate	Events	Rate
BENIN	82	1	1.22	0	0.00	1	1.22	2	2.43
BOTSWANA	95	0	0.00	0	0.00	1	1.05	1	1.05
BURKINA FASO	111	1	0.90	0	0.00	1	0.90	2	1.80
CAMEROON	126	0	0.00	0	0.00	0	0.00	0	0.00
CAPE VERDE**	13	0	0.00	0	0.00	0	0.00	0	0.00
ETHIOPIA	95	0	0.00	0	0.00	3	3.14	3	3.14
GHANA	91	0	0.00	0	0.00	1	1.10	1	1.10
GUINEA	46	1	2.15	0	0.00	2	4.31	3	6.46
KENYA	89	1	1.12	1	1.12	3	3.36	5	5.60
LESOTHO	54	0	0.00	0	0.00	0	0.00	0	0.00
LIBERIA	28	0	0.00	0	0.00	0	0.00	0	0.00
MADAGASCAR	87	0	0.00	0	0.00	0	0.00	0	0.00
MALAWI	71	2	2.82	0	0.00	2	2.82	4	5.64
MALI**	34	0	0.00	0	0.00	0	0.00	0	0.00
MOZAMBIQUE	113	0	0.00	0	0.00	1	0.88	1	0.88
NAMIBIA	82	1	1.23	0	0.00	2	2.45	3	3.68
NIGER**	0	0	0.00	0	0.00	0	0.00	0	0.00
RWANDA	91	1	1.10	0	0.00	0	0.00	1	1.10
SENEGAL	166	1	0.60	0	0.00	4	2.41	5	3.02
SIERRA LEONE	41	2	4.87	0	0.00	0	0.00	2	4.87
SOUTH AFRICA	121	2	1.65	0	0.00	6	4.96	8	6.61
SWAZILAND	48	0	0.00	0	0.00	0	0.00	0	0.00
TANZANIA	106	2	1.89	0	0.00	2	1.89	4	3.78
THE GAMBIA	47	0	0.00	0	0.00	0	0.00	0	0.00
TOGO	60	0	0.00	0	0.00	0	0.00	0	0.00
UGANDA	97	1	1.03	0	0.00	0	0.00	1	1.03
ZAMBIA	170	1	0.59	0	0.00	1	0.59	2	1.18
TOTAL AFRICA	2167	17	0.78	1	0.05	30	1.38	48	2.22

Notes

1.* Peace Corps posts opened or reopened in calendar year 2012: Nepal

2.** Peace Corps posts suspended or closed in calendar year 2012: Cape Verde, Honduras, Mali, Niger, Turkmenistan

3. For Sexual Assaults, incidence rates are per 100 Female VT years.
   For Physical Assaults, Threats, and Property Crimes, incidence rates are per 100 VT years.

Sexual Assault Events and Incidence Rates (2012)
(cont'd)

Global

All Posts	Female VT Years	Rape		Major Sexual Assault		Other Sexual Assault		All Sexual Assault	
		Events	Rate	Events	Rate	Events	Rate	Events	Rate
	4954	31	0.63	9	0.18	125	2.52	165	3.33

EMA Region

Posts	Female VT Years	Rape		Major Sexual Assault		Other Sexual Assault		All Sexual Assault	
		Events	Rate	Events	Rate	Events	Rate	Events	Rate
ALBANIA	49	0	0.00	0	0.00	1	2.05	1	2.05
ARMENIA	55	0	0.00	1	1.81	5	9.03	6	10.84
AZERBAIJAN	67	1	1.50	1	1.50	6	9.00	8	12.00
BULGARIA	50	1	2.02	0	0.00	2	4.04	3	6.06
CAMBODIA	62	1	1.61	0	0.00	0	0.00	1	1.61
CHINA	82	0	0.00	0	0.00	0	0.00	0	0.00
GEORGIA	50	0	0.00	0	0.00	3	6.02	3	6.02
INDONESIA	35	0	0.00	0	0.00	7	19.77	7	19.77
JORDAN	41	0	0.00	0	0.00	2	4.89	2	4.89
KYRGYZ REPUBLIC	43	1	2.32	0	0.00	5	11.59	6	13.91
MACEDONIA	48	0	0.00	0	0.00	1	2.08	1	2.08
MOLDOVA	67	0	0.00	0	0.00	8	11.94	8	11.94
MONGOLIA	66	0	0.00	0	0.00	3	4.54	3	4.54
MOROCCO	157	1	0.64	1	0.64	5	3.19	7	4.47
NEPAL*	3	0	0.00	0	0.00	0	0.00	0	0.00
PHILIPPINES	115	1	0.87	0	0.00	1	0.87	2	1.74
ROMANIA	36	0	0.00	0	0.00	0	0.00	0	0.00
THAILAND	75	0	0.00	1	1.34	2	2.67	3	4.01
TURKMENISTAN**	6	0	0.00	0	0.00	0	0.00	0	0.00
UKRAINE	252	0	0.00	0	0.00	3	1.19	3	1.19
TOTAL EMA	1359	6	0.44	4	0.29	54	3.97	64	4.71

Notes

1.* Peace Corps posts opened or reopened in calendar year 2012: Nepal

2.** Peace Corps posts suspended or closed in calendar year 2012: Cape Verde, Honduras, Mali, Niger, Turkmenistan

3. For Sexual Assaults, incidence rates are per 100 Female VT years.
   For Physical Assaults, Threats, and Property Crimes, incidence rates are per 100 VT years.

Sexual Assault Events and Incidence Rates (2012) (cont'd)

Global

All Posts	Female VT Years	Rape		Major Sexual Assault		Other Sexual Assault		All Sexual Assault	
		Events	Rate	Events	Rate	Events	Rate	Events	Rate
	4954	31	0.63	9	0.18	125	2.52	165	3.33

IAP Region

Posts	Female VT Years	Rape		Major Sexual Assault		Other Sexual Assault		All Sexual Assault	
		Events	Rate	Events	Rate	Events	Rate	Events	Rate
BELIZE	31	0	0.00	0	0.00	0	0.00	0	0.00
COLOMBIA	22	0	0.00	0	0.00	0	0.00	0	0.00
COSTA RICA	85	0	0.00	0	0.00	2	2.36	2	2.36
DOMINICAN REPUBLIC	114	0	0.00	0	0.00	4	3.51	4	3.51
EASTERN CARIBBEAN	70	1	1.44	0	0.00	2	2.87	3	4.31
ECUADOR	126	0	0.00	1	0.79	1	0.79	2	1.59
EL SALVADOR	28	0	0.00	0	0.00	0	0.00	0	0.00
FIJI	24	0	0.00	2	8.31	2	8.31	4	16.63
GUATEMALA	86	0	0.00	0	0.00	7	8.18	7	8.18
GUYANA	53	0	0.00	0	0.00	0	0.00	0	0.00
HONDURAS**	11	0	0.00	0	0.00	0	0.00	0	0.00
JAMAICA	45	1	2.20	0	0.00	0	0.00	1	2.20
MEXICO	37	0	0.00	0	0.00	3	8.17	3	8.17
MICRONESIA	20	0	0.00	0	0.00	0	0.00	0	0.00
NICARAGUA	147	1	0.68	0	0.00	3	2.04	4	2.72
PANAMA	151	1	0.66	0	0.00	4	2.65	5	3.31
PARAGUAY	142	0	0.00	0	0.00	2	1.41	2	1.41
PERU	149	4	2.69	0	0.00	3	2.01	7	4.70
SAMOA	14	0	0.00	0	0.00	1	7.28	1	7.28
SURINAME	24	0	0.00	0	0.00	0	0.00	0	0.00
TONGA	15	0	0.00	1	6.78	1	6.78	2	13.55
VANUATU	36	0	0.00	0	0.00	6	16.87	6	16.87
TOTAL IAP	1428	8	0.56	4	0.28	41	2.87	53	3.71

Notes

1.* Peace Corps posts opened or reopened in calendar year 2012: Nepal

2.** Peace Corps posts suspended or closed in calendar year 2012: Cape Verde, Honduras, Mali, Niger, Turkmenistan

3. For Sexual Assaults, incidence rates are per 100 Female VT years.

For Physical Assaults, Threats, and Property Crimes, incidence rates are per 100 VT years.

Physical Assault Events and Incidence Rates (2012)

Global

All Posts	VT Years	Kidnapping		Aggravated Assault		Major Physical Assault		Other Physical Assault		All Physical Assault	
		Events	Rate	Events	Rate	Events	Rate	Events	Rate	Events	Rate
	8046	3	0.04	15	0.19	8	0.10	80	0.99	106	1.32

Africa Region

Posts	VT Years	Kidnapping		Aggravated Assault		Major Physical Assault		Other Physical Assault		All Physical Assault	
		Events	Rate	Events	Rate	Events	Rate	Events	Rate	Events	Rate
BENIN	121	0	0.00	0	0.00	0	0.00	3	2.47	3	2.47
BOTSWANA	128	0	0.00	1	0.78	0	0.00	1	0.78	2	1.56
BURKINA FASO	172	0	0.00	0	0.00	0	0.00	0	0.00	0	0.00
CAMEROON	198	1	0.51	0	0.00	1	0.51	1	0.51	3	1.52
CAPE VERDE**	31	0	0.00	0	0.00	0	0.00	0	0.00	0	0.00
ETHIOPIA	166	0	0.00	0	0.00	0	0.00	3	1.80	3	1.80
GHANA	172	0	0.00	1	0.58	0	0.00	1	0.58	2	1.16
GUINEA	74	0	0.00	0	0.00	1	1.36	0	0.00	1	1.36
KENYA	134	0	0.00	1	0.74	0	0.00	1	0.74	2	1.49
LESOTHO	73	0	0.00	1	1.36	0	0.00	0	0.00	1	1.36
LIBERIA	57	0	0.00	0	0.00	0	0.00	1	1.74	1	1.74
MADAGASCAR	140	0	0.00	0	0.00	0	0.00	1	0.71	1	0.71
MALAWI	132	0	0.00	0	0.00	0	0.00	1	0.76	1	0.76
MALI**	55	0	0.00	0	0.00	0	0.00	2	3.66	2	3.66
MOZAMBIQUE	163	0	0.00	0	0.00	0	0.00	1	0.61	1	0.61
NAMIBIA	124	1	0.80	0	0.00	0	0.00	1	0.80	2	1.61
NIGER**	0	0	0.00	0	0.00	0	0.00	0	0.00	0	0.00
RWANDA	135	0	0.00	0	0.00	0	0.00	2	1.48	2	1.48
SENEGAL	249	0	0.00	0	0.00	0	0.00	0	0.00	0	0.00
SIERRA LEONE	89	0	0.00	0	0.00	0	0.00	1	1.12	1	1.12
SOUTH AFRICA	179	0	0.00	0	0.00	1	0.56	2	1.11	3	1.67
SWAZILAND	72	0	0.00	0	0.00	0	0.00	0	0.00	0	0.00
TANZANIA	177	0	0.00	2	1.13	0	0.00	0	0.00	2	1.13
THE GAMBIA	83	0	0.00	0	0.00	0	0.00	0	0.00	0	0.00
TOGO	91	0	0.00	0	0.00	0	0.00	1	1.09	1	1.09
UGANDA	157	0	0.00	0	0.00	0	0.00	1	0.64	1	0.64
ZAMBIA	283	0	0.00	0	0.00	0	0.00	2	0.71	2	0.71
TOTAL AFRICA	3460	2	0.06	6	0.17	3	0.09	26	0.75	37	1.07

Notes

1.* Peace Corps posts opened or reopened in calendar year 2012: Nepal

2.** Peace Corps posts suspended or closed in calendar year 2012: Cape Verde, Honduras, Mali, Niger, Turkmenistan

3. For Sexual Assaults, incidence rates are per 100 Female VT years.
   For Physical Assaults, Threats, and Property Crimes, incidence rates are per 100 VT years.

Physical Assault Events and Incidence Rates (2012)
(cont'd)

Global

All Posts	VT Years	Kidnapping		Aggravated Assault		Major Physical Assault		Other Physical Assault		All Physical Assault	
		Events	Rate	Events	Rate	Events	Rate	Events	Rate	Events	Rate
	8046	3	0.04	15	0.19	8	0.10	80	0.99	106	1.32

EMA Region

Posts	VT Years	Kidnapping		Aggravated Assault		Major Physical Assault		Other Physical Assault		All Physical Assault	
		Events	Rate	Events	Rate	Events	Rate	Events	Rate	Events	Rate
ALBANIA	88	0	0.00	1	1.13	1	1.13	2	2.26	4	4.52
ARMENIA	94	0	0.00	0	0.00	0	0.00	0	0.00	0	0.00
AZERBAIJAN	110	0	0.00	0	0.00	1	0.91	3	2.72	4	3.63
BULGARIA	89	0	0.00	0	0.00	0	0.00	3	3.37	3	3.37
CAMBODIA	108	0	0.00	0	0.00	0	0.00	0	0.00	0	0.00
CHINA	153	0	0.00	0	0.00	0	0.00	1	0.65	1	0.65
GEORGIA	83	0	0.00	0	0.00	0	0.00	1	1.21	1	1.21
INDONESIA	63	0	0.00	0	0.00	0	0.00	1	1.58	1	1.58
JORDAN	66	0	0.00	0	0.00	0	0.00	5	7.53	5	7.53
KYRGYZ REPUBLIC	83	0	0.00	0	0.00	0	0.00	5	6.05	5	6.05
MACEDONIA	77	0	0.00	0	0.00	0	0.00	0	0.00	0	0.00
MOLDOVA	118	0	0.00	0	0.00	0	0.00	0	0.00	0	0.00
MONGOLIA	143	0	0.00	2	1.40	1	0.70	3	2.10	6	4.20
MOROCCO	237	0	0.00	0	0.00	0	0.00	6	2.53	6	2.53
NEPAL*	6	0	0.00	0	0.00	0	0.00	0	0.00	0	0.00
PHILIPPINES	186	0	0.00	0	0.00	0	0.00	3	1.61	3	1.61
ROMANIA	63	0	0.00	0	0.00	0	0.00	0	0.00	0	0.00
THAILAND	116	0	0.00	0	0.00	0	0.00	0	0.00	0	0.00
TURKMENISTAN**	14	0	0.00	0	0.00	1	7.01	0	0.00	1	7.01
UKRAINE	432	0	0.00	1	0.23	0	0.00	2	0.46	3	0.69
TOTAL EMA	2331	0	0.00	4	0.17	4	0.17	35	1.50	43	1.84

Notes

1.* Peace Corps posts opened or reopened in calendar year 2012: Nepal

2.** Peace Corps posts suspended or closed in calendar year 2012: Cape Verde, Honduras, Mali, Niger, Turkmenistan

3. For Sexual Assaults, incidence rates are per 100 Female VT years.

   For Physical Assaults, Threats, and Property Crimes, incidence rates are per 100 VT years.

Physical Assault Events and Incidence Rates (2012)
(cont'd)

Global

All Posts	VT Years	Kidnapping		Aggravated Assault		Major Physical Assault		Other Physical Assault		All Physical Assault	
		Events	Rate	Events	Rate	Events	Rate	Events	Rate	Events	Rate
	8046	3	0.04	15	0.19	8	0.10	80	0.99	106	1.32

IAP Region

Posts	VT Years	Kidnapping		Aggravated Assault		Major Physical Assault		Other Physical Assault		All Physical Assault	
		Events	Rate	Events	Rate	Events	Rate	Events	Rate	Events	Rate
BELIZE	42	0	0.00	0	0.00	0	0.00	0	0.00	0	0.00
COLOMBIA	34	0	0.00	0	0.00	0	0.00	3	8.78	3	8.78
COSTA RICA	133	0	0.00	0	0.00	0	0.00	0	0.00	0	0.00
DOMINICAN REPUBLIC	197	0	0.00	0	0.00	0	0.00	2	1.01	2	1.01
EASTERN CARIBBEAN	105	0	0.00	0	0.00	1	0.95	0	0.00	1	0.95
ECUADOR	183	1	0.55	0	0.00	0	0.00	1	0.55	2	1.09
EL SALVADOR	45	0	0.00	0	0.00	0	0.00	0	0.00	0	0.00
FIJI	46	0	0.00	0	0.00	0	0.00	1	2.17	1	2.17
GUATEMALA	119	0	0.00	0	0.00	0	0.00	1	0.84	1	0.84
GUYANA	70	0	0.00	0	0.00	0	0.00	1	1.43	1	1.43
HONDURAS**	19	0	0.00	1	5.28	0	0.00	0	0.00	1	5.28
JAMAICA	69	0	0.00	0	0.00	0	0.00	0	0.00	0	0.00
MEXICO	72	0	0.00	0	0.00	0	0.00	0	0.00	0	0.00
MICRONESIA	30	0	0.00	0	0.00	0	0.00	3	9.86	3	9.86
NICARAGUA	226	0	0.00	0	0.00	0	0.00	0	0.00	0	0.00
PANAMA	241	0	0.00	0	0.00	0	0.00	1	0.41	1	0.41
PARAGUAY	232	0	0.00	1	0.43	0	0.00	5	2.16	6	2.59
PERU	242	0	0.00	2	0.83	0	0.00	0	0.00	2	0.83
SAMOA	21	0	0.00	0	0.00	0	0.00	1	4.76	1	4.76
SURINAME	38	0	0.00	0	0.00	0	0.00	0	0.00	0	0.00
TONGA	23	0	0.00	0	0.00	0	0.00	0	0.00	0	0.00
VANUATU	65	0	0.00	1	1.53	0	0.00	0	0.00	1	1.53
TOTAL IAP	2254	1	0.04	5	0.22	1	0.04	19	0.84	26	1.15

Notes

1.* Peace Corps posts opened or reopened in calendar year 2012: Nepal

2.** Peace Corps posts suspended or closed in calendar year 2012: Cape Verde, Honduras, Mali, Niger, Turkmenistan

3. For Sexual Assaults, incidence rates are per 100 Female VT years.

For Physical Assaults, Threats, and Property Crimes, incidence rates are per 100 VT years.

Threat Events and Incidence Rates (2012)

Global

All Posts	VT Years	Threat	
		Events	Rate
	8046	48	0.60

Africa Region

Posts	VT Years	Threat	
		Events	Rate
BENIN	121	1	0.82
BOTSWANA	128	1	0.78
BURKINA FASO	172	0	0.00
CAMEROON	198	4	2.02
CAPE VERDE**	31	0	0.00
ETHIOPIA	166	0	0.00
GHANA	172	0	0.00
GUINEA	74	0	0.00
KENYA	134	2	1.49
LESOTHO	73	0	0.00
LIBERIA	57	1	1.74
MADAGASCAR	140	0	0.00
MALAWI	132	0	0.00
MALI**	55	0	0.00
MOZAMBIQUE	163	0	0.00
NAMIBIA	124	2	1.61
NIGER**	0	0	0.00
RWANDA	135	1	0.74
SENEGAL	249	0	0.00
SIERRA LEONE	89	1	1.12
SOUTH AFRICA	179	2	1.11
SWAZILAND	72	1	1.39
TANZANIA	177	0	0.00
THE GAMBIA	83	0	0.00
TOGO	91	0	0.00
UGANDA	157	2	1.27
ZAMBIA	283	2	0.71
TOTAL AFRICA	3460	20	0.58

Notes

1.* Peace Corps posts opened or reopened in calendar year 2012: Nepal

2.** Peace Corps posts suspended or closed in calendar year 2012: Cape Verde, Honduras, Mali, Niger, Turkmenistan

3. For Sexual Assaults, incidence rates are per 100 Female VT years.
   For Physical Assaults, Threats, and Property Crimes, incidence rates are per 100 VT years.

Threat Events and Incidence Rates (2012)
(cont'd)

Global

All Posts	VT Years	Threat	
		Events	Rate
	8046	48	0.60

EMA Region

Posts	VT Years	Threat	
		Events	Rate
ALBANIA	88	0	0.00
ARMENIA	94	0	0.00
AZERBAIJAN	110	0	0.00
BULGARIA	89	2	2.24
CAMBODIA	108	1	0.92
CHINA	153	0	0.00
GEORGIA	83	0	0.00
INDONESIA	63	1	1.58
JORDAN	66	0	0.00
KYRGYZ REPUBLIC	83	1	1.21
MACEDONIA	77	0	0.00
MOLDOVA	118	0	0.00
MONGOLIA	143	0	0.00
MOROCCO	237	1	0.42
NEPAL*	6	0	0.00
PHILIPPINES	186	1	0.54
ROMANIA	63	0	0.00
THAILAND	116	1	0.86
TURKMENISTAN**	14	1	7.01
UKRAINE	432	0	0.00
TOTAL EMA	2331	9	0.39

Notes

1.* Peace Corps posts opened or reopened in calendar year 2012: Nepal

2.** Peace Corps posts suspended or closed in calendar year 2012: Cape Verde, Honduras, Mali, Niger, Turkmenistan

3. For Sexual Assaults, incidence rates are per 100 Female VT years.
   For Physical Assaults, Threats, and Property Crimes, incidence rates are per 100 VT years.

Threat Events and Incidence Rates (2012)
(cont'd)

Global

All Posts	VT Years	Threat	
		Events	Rate
	8046	48	0.60

IAP Region

Posts	VT Years	Threat	
		Events	Rate
BELIZE	42	1	2.36
COLOMBIA	34	1	2.93
COSTA RICA	133	0	0.00
DOMINICAN REPUBLIC	197	1	0.51
EASTERN CARIBBEAN	105	3	2.85
ECUADOR	183	0	0.00
EL SALVADOR	45	0	0.00
FIJI	46	2	4.34
GUATEMALA	119	0	0.00
GUYANA	70	1	1.43
HONDURAS**	19	0	0.00
JAMAICA	69	0	0.00
MEXICO	72	1	1.39
MICRONESIA	30	0	0.00
NICARAGUA	226	2	0.89
PANAMA	241	0	0.00
PARAGUAY	232	3	1.29
PERU	242	0	0.00
SAMOA	21	1	4.76
SURINAME	38	0	0.00
TONGA	23	0	0.00
VANUATU	65	3	4.58
TOTAL IAP	2254	19	0.84

Notes

1.* Peace Corps posts opened or reopened in calendar year 2012: Nepal

2.** Peace Corps posts suspended or closed in calendar year 2012: Cape Verde, Honduras, Mali, Niger, Turkmenistan

3. For Sexual Assaults, incidence rates are per 100 Female VT years.
   For Physical Assaults, Threats, and Property Crimes, incidence rates are per 100 VT years.

Property Crime Events and Incidence Rates (2012)

Global

All Posts	VT Years	Robbery		Burglary		Theft		Vandalism		All Property Crime	
		Events	Rate	Events	Rate	Events	Rate	Events	Rate	Events	Rate
	8046	155	1.93	328	4.08	779	9.68	1	0.01	1263	15.70

Africa Region

Posts	VT Years	Robbery		Burglary		Theft		Vandalism		All Property Crime	
		Events	Rate	Events	Rate	Events	Rate	Events	Rate	Events	Rate
BENIN	121	4	3.29	9	7.41	10	8.24	0	0.00	23	18.94
BOTSWANA	128	6	4.68	12	9.35	3	2.34	0	0.00	21	16.36
BURKINA FASO	172	0	0.00	10	5.82	20	11.64	0	0.00	30	17.46
CAMEROON	198	5	2.53	11	5.56	13	6.57	0	0.00	29	14.66
CAPE VERDE**	31	2	6.42	1	3.21	0	0.00	0	0.00	3	9.63
ETHIOPIA	166	1	0.60	8	4.81	30	18.03	0	0.00	39	23.45
GHANA	172	1	0.58	15	8.71	7	4.06	0	0.00	23	13.35
GUINEA	74	1	1.36	4	5.44	0	0.00	0	0.00	5	6.79
KENYA	134	2	1.49	6	4.46	15	11.16	0	0.00	23	17.11
LESOTHO	73	1	1.36	1	1.36	10	13.61	0	0.00	12	16.33
LIBERIA	57	2	3.49	5	8.71	9	15.68	0	0.00	16	27.88
MADAGASCAR	140	5	3.56	20	14.24	23	16.37	0	0.00	48	34.17
MALAWI	132	2	1.52	10	7.59	20	15.17	0	0.00	32	24.27
MALI**	55	1	1.83	1	1.83	7	12.82	0	0.00	9	16.49
MOZAMBIQUE	163	5	3.06	14	8.57	4	2.45	0	0.00	23	14.07
NAMIBIA	124	3	2.41	16	12.86	26	20.90	0	0.00	45	36.17
NIGER**	0	0	0.00	0	0.00	0	0.00	0	0.00	0	0.00
RWANDA	135	1	0.74	12	8.87	10	7.39	0	0.00	23	17.00
SENEGAL	249	6	2.41	11	4.42	18	7.23	0	0.00	35	14.06
SIERRA LEONE	89	4	4.49	6	6.74	18	20.22	0	0.00	28	31.45
SOUTH AFRICA	179	13	7.24	7	3.90	23	12.82	0	0.00	43	23.96
SWAZILAND	72	1	1.39	0	0.00	5	6.94	0	0.00	6	8.33
TANZANIA	177	3	1.69	5	2.82	4	2.25	0	0.00	12	6.76
THE GAMBIA	83	2	2.40	6	7.21	3	3.60	0	0.00	11	13.21
TOGO	91	2	2.19	3	3.28	3	3.28	0	0.00	8	8.75
UGANDA	157	1	0.64	11	6.99	17	10.80	0	0.00	29	18.43
ZAMBIA	283	3	1.06	9	3.17	28	9.88	0	0.00	40	14.11
TOTAL AFRICA	3460	77	2.23	213	6.16	326	9.42	0	0.00	616	17.80

Notes

1.* Peace Corps posts opened or reopened in calendar year 2012: Nepal

2.** Peace Corps posts suspended or closed in calendar year 2012: Cape Verde, Honduras, Mali, Niger, Turkmenistan

3. For Sexual Assaults, incidence rates are per 100 Female VT years.
    For Physical Assaults, Threats, and Property Crimes, incidence rates are per 100 VT years.

Property Crime Events and Incidence Rates (2012)
(cont'd)

Global

All Posts	VT Years	Robbery		Burglary		Theft		Vandalism		All Property Crime	
		Events	Rate	Events	Rate	Events	Rate	Events	Rate	Events	Rate
	8046	155	1.93	328	4.08	779	9.68	1	0.01	1263	15.70

EMA Region

Posts	VT Years	Robbery		Burglary		Theft		Vandalism		All Property Crime	
		Events	Rate	Events	Rate	Events	Rate	Events	Rate	Events	Rate
ALBANIA	88	1	1.13	2	2.26	6	6.79	0	0.00	9	10.18
ARMENIA	94	0	0.00	2	2.12	0	0.00	0	0.00	2	2.12
AZERBAIJAN	110	1	0.91	0	0.00	2	1.82	0	0.00	3	2.72
BULGARIA	89	0	0.00	1	1.12	8	8.97	0	0.00	9	10.10
CAMBODIA	108	1	0.92	1	0.92	26	24.05	0	0.00	28	25.90
CHINA	153	0	0.00	1	0.65	9	5.89	0	0.00	10	6.54
GEORGIA	83	0	0.00	0	0.00	2	2.41	0	0.00	2	2.41
INDONESIA	63	2	3.16	0	0.00	4	6.32	0	0.00	6	9.48
JORDAN	66	0	0.00	3	4.52	3	4.52	0	0.00	6	9.03
KYRGYZ REPUBLIC	83	1	1.21	1	1.21	6	7.26	0	0.00	8	9.68
MACEDONIA	77	0	0.00	0	0.00	5	6.46	0	0.00	5	6.46
MOLDOVA	118	2	1.69	0	0.00	5	4.23	0	0.00	7	5.92
MONGOLIA	143	1	0.70	2	1.40	18	12.59	0	0.00	21	14.69
MOROCCO	237	5	2.11	2	0.84	17	7.18	0	0.00	24	10.13
NEPAL*	6	0	0.00	0	0.00	1	15.61	0	0.00	1	15.61
PHILIPPINES	186	3	1.61	5	2.69	35	18.84	1	0.54	44	23.68
ROMANIA	63	1	1.60	1	1.60	4	6.40	0	0.00	6	9.60
THAILAND	116	0	0.00	2	1.72	5	4.30	0	0.00	7	6.03
TURKMENISTAN**	14	0	0.00	0	0.00	2	14.02	0	0.00	2	14.02
UKRAINE	432	0	0.00	1	0.23	29	6.71	0	0.00	30	6.94
TOTAL EMA	2331	18	0.77	24	1.03	187	8.02	1	0.04	230	9.87

Notes

1.* Peace Corps posts opened or reopened in calendar year 2012: Nepal

2.** Peace Corps posts suspended or closed in calendar year 2012: Cape Verde, Honduras, Mali, Niger, Turkmenistan

3. For Sexual Assaults, incidence rates are per 100 Female VT years.

For Physical Assaults, Threats, and Property Crimes, incidence rates are per 100 VT years.

Property Crime Events and Incidence Rates (2012)
(cont'd)

Global

All Posts	VT Years	Robbery		Burglary		Theft		Vandalism		All Property Crime	
		Events	Rate	Events	Rate	Events	Rate	Events	Rate	Events	Rate
	8046	155	1.93	328	4.08	779	9.68	1	0.01	1263	15.70

IAP Region

Posts	VT Years	Robbery		Burglary		Theft		Vandalism		All Property Crime	
		Events	Rate	Events	Rate	Events	Rate	Events	Rate	Events	Rate
BELIZE	42	1	2.36	3	7.09	5	11.81	0	0.00	9	21.26
COLOMBIA	34	4	11.70	0	0.00	18	52.65	0	0.00	22	64.36
COSTA RICA	133	9	6.77	6	4.51	21	15.79	0	0.00	36	27.06
DOMINICAN REPUBLIC	197	4	2.03	7	3.55	16	8.11	0	0.00	27	13.68
EASTERN CARIBBEAN	105	2	1.90	9	8.54	9	8.54	0	0.00	20	18.98
ECUADOR	183	9	4.91	2	1.09	12	6.54	0	0.00	23	12.54
EL SALVADOR	45	2	4.43	2	4.43	3	6.65	0	0.00	7	15.51
FIJI	46	0	0.00	8	17.35	7	15.18	0	0.00	15	32.53
GUATEMALA	119	3	2.53	5	4.21	24	20.20	0	0.00	32	26.93
GUYANA	70	3	4.30	2	2.87	5	7.17	0	0.00	10	14.33
HONDURAS**	19	0	0.00	0	0.00	0	0.00	0	0.00	0	0.00
JAMAICA	69	0	0.00	3	4.33	3	4.33	0	0.00	6	8.65
MEXICO	72	0	0.00	1	1.39	5	6.94	0	0.00	6	8.32
MICRONESIA	30	0	0.00	5	16.43	2	6.57	0	0.00	7	23.01
NICARAGUA	226	4	1.77	4	1.77	31	13.73	0	0.00	39	17.28
PANAMA	241	4	1.66	6	2.49	16	6.64	0	0.00	26	10.79
PARAGUAY	232	7	3.02	14	6.03	34	14.65	0	0.00	55	23.71
PERU	242	6	2.48	4	1.65	39	16.13	0	0.00	49	20.26
SAMOA	21	0	0.00	1	4.76	3	14.27	0	0.00	4	19.03
SURINAME	38	0	0.00	3	7.95	2	5.30	0	0.00	5	13.26
TONGA	23	1	4.27	1	4.27	1	4.27	0	0.00	3	12.81
VANUATU	65	1	1.53	5	7.64	10	15.28	0	0.00	16	24.44
TOTAL IAP	2254	60	2.66	91	4.04	266	11.80	0	0.00	417	18.50

Notes

1.* Peace Corps posts opened or reopened in calendar year 2012: Nepal

2.** Peace Corps posts suspended or closed in calendar year 2012: Cape Verde, Honduras, Mali, Niger, Turkmenistan

3. For Sexual Assaults, incidence rates are per 100 Female VT years.

   For Physical Assaults, Threats, and Property Crimes, incidence rates are per 100 VT years.

Volunteers serving in . . .	Also reported . . .
Albania	Theft in Greece*
Azerbaijan	Robbery in Georgia
	Rape/Attempted Rape in Turkey*
Benin	Theft in Burkina Faso
Bulgaria	Theft in Macedonia
Colombia	Other Physical Assault in Panama
Dominican Republic	Theft in Guatemala
El Salvador	Robbery in Guatemala
Guatemala	Theft in Brazil*
Jamaica	Rape/Attempted Rape in the United States*
Jordan	Theft in Ukraine
Lesotho	Robbery and 2 Thefts in South Africa
	Theft in the United States*
Macedonia	Theft in Croatia*
Madagascar	Robbery in Senegal
Mali	Other Physical Assault in Cape Verde
	2 Thefts in Ghana
Moldova	Robbery, Other Sexual Assault and
	Theft in Ukraine
Mozambique	Robbery in South Africa
Namibia	Rape/Attempted Rape and Robbery in Mozambique
	2 Thefts in Zambia
Panama	Theft in Colombia
Paraguay	4 Thefts in Argentina*
	Theft in Peru
Rwanda	Theft in Tanzania
	Rape/Attempted Rape in Uganda
Swaziland	Robbery and Theft in South Africa
Togo	Robbery in Ghana
Uganda	Theft in South Africa
	Robbery in Tanzania
Zambia	Theft in Namibia
	Theft in South Africa

*Not a current Peace Corps post.

Note: In 2012, 43 incidents occurred in a country other than the Volunteer's post of service. Of the 43 incidents, 10 occurred in a country that is not a current Peace Corps post.